# IN PRAISE OF
# GOLF

*"Golf, to the man or woman who regards it simply as a game, will remain for ever insoluble and an enigma, and it will retain its greatness because it contains something that lifts it higher than that of a mere pastime."*—J.H. TAYLOR

# IN PRAISE OF GOLF

*An Anthology for all Lovers of the Game*

COMPILED BY
## WEBSTER EVANS
AND
## TOM SCOTT
*Editor of "Golf Illustrated"*

ABERCROMBIE & FITCH

## LIBRARY

BOOKSELLERS
EST. 1892

First published in Great Britain by Frederick Mueller Ltd. in 1950
and reprinted in the United States of America for Abercrombie &
Fitch, Inc. by Rutledge Hill Press, 513 Third Avenue South,
Nashville, Tennessee.

ISBN: 1-55853-152-1

Printed in United States of America

1 2 3 4 5 6 7 8 — 97 96 95 94 93 92 91

# THE FREEMASONRY OF GOLF

GOLF may be, and is, used by people of every colour, race, creed and temperament, in every climate and all the year round. No recreation, apart from the simplest contests of the river and field, has been so universal since the world began, with the single exception of chess. And wherever and whenever it is played, it extends its benign influence towards the promotion of fast friendship among the players. There is no freemasonry like the freemasonry of golf. To its temples in every land are always welcomed the faithful and earnest craftsman from where'er he came, and he is passed on the signs of the bag and the stance and the little pimpled ball. For it is one of the articles of belief that no man can be a good and enthusiastic golfer of experience and at the same time a thoroughly bad fellow, for at the outset of his career the bad fellow would never be happy in his game. . . . Thus has our happy game of golf wound a bright cordon round the world, and so does she play her part in the great evolution of general contentment.

HENRY LEACH.

# THE UNIVERSAL GAME

GOLF is a game for the many. It suits all sorts and conditions of men—the strong and the weak, the halt and the maimed, the octogenarian and the boy, the rich and the poor, the clergyman and the infidel. . . . The late riser can play comfortably and be back for his rubber in the afternoon; the sanguine man can measure himself against those who will beat him; the half-crown seeker can find victims; the gambler can bet; the man of high principle, by playing for nothing, may enjoy himself and yet feel good. You can brag, and lose matches; depreciate yourself, and win them. Unlike the other Scotch game of whisky-drinking, excess in it is not injurious to the health.

SIR WALTER SIMPSON.

GOLF is the only game where the worst player gets the best of it. He obtains more out of it as regards both exercise and enjoyment, for the good player gets worried over the slightest mistake, whereas the poor player makes too many mistakes to worry over them.

DAVID LLOYD GEORGE.

SUNNINGDALE, BERKSHIRE

*One of the finest inland courses in England; the fourth green, with the fifth and sixth holes beyond*

GOLF is the peculiar game of a peculiar people; its trend is onward on parallel lines; it is the pastime of the Scots.

JOHN L. LOW.

GOLF may be played on Sunday, not being a game within the view of the law, but being a form of moral effort.

STEPHEN LEACOCK.

GOLF is not a wrestle with Bogey; it is not a struggle with your mortal foe; it is a physiological, psychological, and moral fight with yourself; it is a test of mastery over self; and the ultimate and irreducible element of the game is to determine which of the players is the more worthy combatant.

ARNOLD HAULTAIN.

# IT ALL DEPENDS . . .

GOLF is a test of temper, a trial of honour, a revealer of character. It affords a chance to play the man and act the gentleman. It means going into God's out-of-doors, getting close to nature, fresh air, exercise, a sweeping away of the mental cobwebs, genuine re-creation of the tired tissues. It is a cure for care—an antidote to worry. It includes companionship with friends, social intercourse, opportunities for courtesy, kindliness and generosity to an opponent. It promotes not only physical health but moral force.

DAVID ROBERTSON FORGAN.

GOLF increases the blood pressure, ruins the disposition, spoils the digestion, induces neurasthenia, hurts the eyes, callouses the hands, ties kinks in the nervous system, debauches the morals, drives men to drink or homicide, breaks up the family, turns the ductless glands into internal warts, corrodes the pneumogastric nerve, breaks off the edges of the vertebrae, induces spinal meningitis and progressive mendacity, and starts angina pectoris.

DR. A. S. LAMB (*McGill University*).

# GOLF IN HISTORY

IT answers to a rustic pastime of the Romans, which they played with a ball of leather stuffed with feathers, called Paganica, and the goff-ball is composed of the same materials to this day. In the reign of Edward the Third the Latin name, Cambuca, was applied to this pastime, and it derived the denomination, no doubt, from the crooked club or bat with which it was played.

JOSEPH STRUTT (1749-1803).
*From "Sports and Pastimes*
*of the People of England."*

THAT golf is of considerable antiquity there is no reasonable ground to doubt; and as the best proof of this, it may be mentioned that there are statutes of so early a date as the year 1457, prohibiting the exercise of golf, lest it should interfere with the more important accomplishment of archery (in Scotland). . . .

In 1491 it is statute and ordained: "That in na place of the realme there be usit futte-ballis, golfe, or uther sik unprofitabill sportis, for the commoun gude of the realme, and defence thairof."

JOHN CUNDELL.
*From "Some Historical Notices Relative to the*
*Progress of the Game of Golf in Scotland" (1824).*

# "AUTRES TEMPS, AUTRES MŒURS"

FEB. 11, 1608. The which day compeirit John Henrie, Pat. Bogie, James Kid, George Robertsoune, and James Watsoune, and being accusit for playing of the gowff everie Sabboth the tyme of the sermonnes, notwithstanding oft admonitioun past befoir, were convict of xx. lib. ilk ane of them, and ordainit to be wardet (put in prison) until the same were payit, and to find cautioun not to do the lyke again at na tyme heireafter, under the paine of c. lib.

*From the Register of the Kirk Session of North Leith.*

THUS all our life long we are frolick and gay, And instead of Court revels, we merrily play At Trap, at Rules, and at Barly-break run: At Goff, and at Foot-ball, and when we have done These innocent sports, we'll laugh and lie down, And to each pretty lass We will give a green Gown.

THOMAS SHADWELL.
*A Song from the Play "Westminster Drollery" (1671).*

11

# A FAMOUS EDINBURGH GOLFER

WILLIAM ST. CLAIR of Roslin, a famous eighteenth-century golfer and Captain of the Honourable Company of Edinburgh Golfers, is thus described by Sir Walter Scott in *Provincial Antiquities*:

"A man considerably above six feet, with dark-grey locks, a form upright, but gracefully so, thin-flanked and broad-shouldered, built, it would seem, for the business of the war or the chase; a noble eye of chastened pride and undoubting authority, and features handsome and striking in their general effect, though somewhat harsh and exaggerated when considered in detail. His complexion was dark and grizzled, and, as we schoolboys who crowded to see him perform feats of strength and skill in the old Scottish games of golf and archery used to think and say amongst ourselves, the whole figure resembled the famous founder of the Douglas race."

SIR WALTER SCOTT.

WILLIAM ST. CLAIR OF ROSLIN

*An eighteenth-century Captain of the Honourable
Company of Edinburgh Golfers whom Sir Walter
Scott saw playing*

# LEITH LINKS

NORTH from *Edina* eight furlongs and more
    Lies that fam'd field, on *Fortha's* sounding
        shore.
Here, *Caledonian* Chiefs for health resort,
Confirm their sinews by the manly sport.
*Macdonald* and unmatch'd *Dalrymple* ply
Their pond'rous weapons, and the green defy;
*Rattray* for skill, and *Crosse* for strength renown'd,
*Stuart* and *Leslie* beat the sandy ground,
And *Brown* and *Alston*, Chiefs well known to fame,
And numbers more the Muse forbears to name.
Gigantic *Biggar* here full oft is seen,
Like huge behemoth on an *Indian* green;
His bulk enormous scarce can 'scape the eyes,
Amaz'd spectators wonder how he plies.
Yea, here great *Forbes*, patron of the just,
The dread of villains and the good man's trust,
When spent with toils in serving human kind,
His body recreates, and unbends his mind.

THOMAS MATHISON.
*From "The Goff"* (1743).

# SMOLLETT ON GOLF

IN the fields called the Links, the citizens of Edinburgh divert themselves at a game called Golf, in which they use a curious kind of bats tipped with horn, and small elastic balls of leather, stuffed with feathers. . . . These they strike with such force and dexterity from one hole to another, that they will fly to an incredible distance. Of this diversion the Scots are so fond that, when the weather will permit, you may see a multitude of all ranks, from the senator of justice to the lowest tradesman, mingled together, in their shirts, and following the balls with the utmost eagerness. Among others, I was shown one particular set of golfers, the youngest of whom was turned fourscore. They were all gentlemen of independent fortunes, who had amused themselves with this pastime for the best part of a century, without having ever felt the least alarm from sickness or disgust; and they never went to bed without having each the best part of a gallon of claret in his belly. Such uninterrupted exercise, co-operating with the keen air from the sea, must, without all doubt, keep the appetite always on edge, and steel the constitution against all the common attacks of distemper.

TOBIAS SMOLLETT (1721-71).
*From "Humphrey Clinker."*

# ALLAN ROBERTSON
## (1815-1859)

WHO shall describe his elegant and beautifully correct style of play? The champion was remarkable for his *easy* style, depending on a long cool swing, and never on sheer strength. His clubs were of the *toy* description, as the slang of the Links hath it, possessing no weight or misproportion of wood. Indeed, in a word, Allan's game throughout was pure unadulterated science. No man, perhaps, so well united in his play all the bits of the game. . . .

His coolness was unique, and almost miraculous. He was never known to *funk* or indeed change his off-hand manner in the least. He was never beaten—proud epitaph. It is something to be the best in anything, of all the world, and Allan stood confessed the model player. But it is not only as a golfer that Allan is to be deeply deplored. He was possessed of the best heart and kindliest feelings in the world. In the intricate dealings of the Links, in the formation and playing of great matches, Allan was honourable, just and gentlemanly, from first to last.

*From the "Dundee Advertiser" (September, 1859).*

# ADDRESS TO ST. ANDREWS

ST. ANDREWS! they say that thy glories are
  gone,
 That thy streets are deserted, thy castles o'er-
   thrown:
If thy glories *be* gone, they are only, methinks,
As it were, by enchantment, transferr'd to thy Links.
Though thy streets be not now, as of yore, full of
  prelates,
Of abbots and monks, and of hot-headed zealots,
Let none judge us rashly, or blame us as scoffers,
When we say that instead there are Links full of
  Golfers,
With more of good heart and good feeling among
  them
Than the abbots, the monks, and the zealots who
  sung them:
We have red coats and bonnets, we've putters and
  clubs;
The green has its bunkers, its hazards, and rubs;
At the long hole across we have biscuits and beer,
And the Hebes who sell it give zest to the cheer:
If this makes not up for the pomp and the splendour
Of mitres, and murders, and mass—we'll surrender;
If Golfers and caddies be not better neighbours

Than abbots and soldiers with crosses and sabres,
Let such fancies remain with the fool who so thinks,
While we toast old St. Andrews, its Golfers and
    Links.

GEORGE FULLERTON CARNEGIE.
*From "Golfiana" (1833).*


## THE UNIQUE "OLD COURSE"

IF I am asked which is my favourite course, I
give my answer unhesitatingly—the Old Course
at St. Andrews. I think it is the best, and if I
have got to play a match which is really of some
importance, that is where I want to play it. St.
Andrews has got a character and features that you
find nowhere else. What I like about it is this, that
you may play a very good shot there and find
yourself in a very bad place. That is the real game
of golf. I don't want everything levelled and
smoothed away so that by no possible chance can
your ball take an unlucky turn in a direction you
don't like. People think and talk too much about
"fairness."

GEORGE DUNCAN.

THE EIGHTEENTH GREEN AT ST. ANDREWS

*In the background, the clubhouse of the Royal and Ancient Golf Club.*
*A photograph taken during the Walker Cup match in 1947*

# A MATCH FOR £400

IN 1849 a match for £400 was played between Allan Robertson and Tom Morris against the brothers Dunn of Musselburgh, over the last-named green, St. Andrews and North Berwick. Over their own green the brothers made a terrible example of the St. Andrews couple, winning by 13 and 12 to play. The latter, however, by a narrow majority, reversed the result at St. Andrews, leaving the final battle to be fought at North Berwick. . . .

It would be difficult to find in the whole annals of golf a more perfect illustration of the advantages of pluck and perseverance. The winners, as they unexpectedly turned out to be, halved the first round at North Berwick, lost the second by four, and halved the third; at the fourth hole of the last round were still further astern, being no less than five down, and their position became worse when four down and eight to play was announced.

Odds of twenty to one were freely laid on the Dunns; but here began a most extraordinary run of surprises, for Allan and Tom won the first hole, then the second, halved the third, won the fourth, halved the fifth, and won the sixth; all square and two to play. Amid breathless excitement, Tom played a fine tee shot which, however, was not well followed up by his partner; the brothers, however, by pulling their second shot off the course, landed under a large boulder, and thus lost the hole. So Tom and his partner, retaining their advantage, pulled this remarkable match out of the fire, and landed the £400, to say nothing of the twenty to one odds which had been laid when their condition appeared hopeless.

H. S. C. EVERARD.

"PUIR Allan! The cunningest bit body o' a player, I dae think, that iver haun'led cleek an' putter. An' a kindly body, tae, as it weel does fit me to say, an' wi' a wealth o' slee pawky fun aboot him."

TOM MORRIS *on his old master.*

# YOUNG TOMMY'S LAST GAMES

THE last important foursome in which Tommy Morris was engaged took place in September, 1875, when, in conjunction with his father, he played Willie and Mungo Park over North Berwick for £25 a side. The Morrises won a very close tussle, amidst considerable excitement, by one hole. . . .

In connection with this match a sad incident occurred: when the last hole had been played out, a telegram was handed to young Tom, requesting him to return home at once as his wife was dangerously ill. No train being then available, Tommy and his father started off in a yacht which had been kindly placed at their disposal. They had barely cleared the harbour when another message arrived, announcing that young Mrs. Morris and her new-born baby were both dead. There can be no doubt that the young champion never recovered from this blow, for he was devotedly attached to his wife, to whom he had only been married about a year.

One more important match he played before his death. Mr. Arthur Molesworth of Westward Ho! had announced that, on receipt of a third, he was prepared to play any professional; and this challenge

Tommy was induced to accept. Two rounds a day for three days over St. Andrews was quite sufficient to prove Tommy's great superiority even at the odds conceded, and by the decisive majority of nine up and seven to play he defeated the southern representative. During a great portion of the match the links were covered with snow. . . . Very shortly after this, on Christmas Day, 1875, at the age of twenty-four, this grand golfer passed away lamented by all who knew him.

H. S. C. EVERARD.

"I COULD cope wi' Allan masel', but never wi' Tommy."

"OLD TOM" MORRIS on his son.

"I CAN'T imagine anyone playing better than Tommy did."

LESLIE BALFOUR-MELVILLE, who often played with Tommy Morris.

# THE HEIRLOOM

THE Championship Belt was played for in the early days. Willie Park won it on three different occasions, and I won it on four, but not year after year. Then my son Tommy was the winner of it for three years running (1868, 1869 and 1870), and it became his own property for good. I have the belt in my house now, and it is the proudest possession that I have—in my eyes it is absolutely priceless. It is composed of a big, broad belt of dark red morocco leather, with rich golfing designs in silver upon it as ornaments.

I could also show you two photographs—extremely interesting and valuable to me—of my two sons, Tommy and Jimmy. They are in one frame, and underneath the pictures are printed their best scores round St. Andrews links, and curiously enough the totals are exactly the same—77. Tommy did it in 1869, going out in 37 strokes and returning in 40, and in 1887 Jimmy went out in 38 and came home in 39, both 77.

"OLD TOM" MORRIS.

## "OLD TOM" MORRIS

*The professional at St. Andrews from 1865 until 1904,
whose bearded features are famous wherever golf is played*

# AN ALL-TIME RECORD!

IN the late eighteen-nineties, golf was beginning to interest the London Press. To this was owing the father of all the fast time stories. Jack White did 75 in his last round. A message transmitted to one of the London evening papers: "White went round in 75—a record," fell into the hands of a sports' sub-editor who, ignorant of golf, caught a "stop-press" box with the intelligence that Jack White had "broken record at Sandwich, going round in 7 minutes 5 seconds."

WILLIAM REID.

## "ANDRA" KIRKALDY

IT would take a volume in itself to set out the Kirkaldy stories. His partnerships with "Wee Ben" Sayers are among the immortal memories of golf. They were a pawky pair, and they were always sure of a good many laughs on the way round. . . . Kirkaldy had to play a stroke from the railway at St. Andrews in the days when the railway was not out of bounds. "Andra" went over and studied the lie of the ball. "Lend me yer wee mashie," he called to Ben. "Na, na," replied Ben. "Brek yer ain club!"

FRANK MORAN.

26

# GOLF FOR WOMEN—1890 VERSION

WE have always advocated a liberal exten-
sion of the right of golfing to women. Not
many years ago their position was most
degraded. . . . We therefore gladly welcomed the
establishment of ladies' links—a kind of Jews'
quarter—which have now been generously pro-
vided for them on most of the larger greens.

Ladies' links should be laid out on the model,
though on a smaller scale, of the "long round";
containing some short putting holes, some longer
holes, admitting of a drive or two of seventy or
eighty yards, and a few suitable hazards. We
venture to suggest seventy or eighty yards as the
average limit of a drive advisedly; not because
we doubt a lady's power to make a longer drive,
but because that cannot well be done without
raising the club above the shoulder. Now, we do
not presume to dictate, but we must observe that
the posture and gestures requisite for a full swing
are not particularly graceful when the player is
clad in female dress.

LORD WELLWOOD (1890).

# THE LADIES' GREEN, ST. ANDREWS

OF late years the ladies, as an improvement on such drivelling games as croquet and lawn-billiards, have taken vigorously to Golf; and the Ladies' Green at St. Andrews is now a very charming feature of the place. On occasion of playing for prizes, a very large field turns out; and when the day is reasonably propitious, the sun being gallant enough to light up for us the fancy costumes, a prettier and gayer sight is not readily to be found. The skill of the fair competitors is by no means to be despised; and on their own ground the best of them would be backed freely against the "Cracks" of the Royal and Ancient.

*From "Golf: A Royal and Ancient Game" (1893).*

# "MISS HIGGINS"

HOW on earth any one of us (in the 'nineties) ever managed to hit a ball, or get along at all, in the outrageous garments with which fashion decreed we were to cover ourselves, is one of the great unsolved mysteries of that or any age. . . . I can remember when the sleeves were so voluminous that we always had to have an elastic strap round the left arm, or we should never have seen the ball at all. "Miss Higgins" (named after the American golfer) was indispensable on account of the width of the skirts. "Miss Higgins" was an elastic band, which was slipped round the knees when the player was addressing her ball, and was the most useful as well as the most unsightly of the many inventions to counteract the vagaries and inconsistencies of *la mode*. . . .

The golfing girl of to-day should indeed be grateful that she need not play golf in a sailor hat, a high stiff collar, a voluminous skirt and petticoats, a motor-veil, or a wide skirt with leather binding.

MABEL E. STRINGER.

# A SHOCK FOR THE STRANGER

DURING the morning round in the final of the Ladies' Championship in 1928, Glenna Collett, the famous American player, was five up on Joyce Wethered, the subsequent winner.

A stranger, quite indifferent to golf, who was walking in the streets of St. Andrews bent on seeing the Cathedral and the University, was surprised to find himself addressed by a postman in a depressed tone of voice, as he passed gloomily on his rounds, with the remark: "She's five doon." What the stranger thought of this unsolicited piece of information, I cannot imagine.

JOYCE WETHERED.

EACH of the two, Bobby Jones and Miss Joyce Wethered, are in the class of game-playing geniuses that only arise once in a very long while. In the nineteenth century there was young Tommy Morris, I suppose—it can only be a matter of hearsay—and, I am quite sure, Harry Vardon. In the twentieth, as far as it has gone, their successors seem to be clear.

BERNARD DARWIN.

JOYCE WETHERED (LADY HEATHCOAT-AMORY)

*The world's greatest lady golfer*

# BUNKER ETIQUETTE

WHEN you find the bunker, mind you
Fill the holes wherein you stand.
Don't depart and leave behind you
Footprints in the silver sand.
Footprints which, unless you smother,
By some other may be found;
He'll say something worse than "Bother!"
If you spoil his medal round.

GERALD BATCHELOR.

## COMPENSATION

CHARLES HAWTREY, the actor, was playing golf one day and was bunkered at the first hole. While he was trying to extricate his ball, his caddie took out a clay pipe and began to fill it. At Hawtrey's fifteenth stroke the caddie struck a match on his trousers. Hawtrey paused in his efforts and looked at him.

"Well," said the caddie, "it's a fine day, anyway."

# "THE TEARS OF BEARDED MEN . . ."

IN the last round of the Open Championship at Prestwick in 1890, John Ball, who won it, was playing with Willy Campbell, splendid player, most gallant of match fighters, certainly deserving of championship honours and only missing them by one of those fatal accidents, very near home. . . . Poor Willy on that occasion got heavily bunkered, lost his head a little and perhaps his temper more than a little. He had strokes to spare; but he wasted them hammering in that bunker, and when I came into Charlie Hunter's shop at Prestwick half an hour later I saw a sad sight. Willy Campbell was sitting on an upturned bucket on one side of the door, his caddie had a similar humble seat on the other side of the door—and both were weeping bitterly.

HORACE HUTCHINSON.

THE game is not so easy as it seems. In the first place, the terrible *inertia* of the ball must be overcome.

LORD WELLWOOD.

# A GREAT FINAL

IN the Amateur Championship of 1899 at Prestwick, John Ball stood one up with two to play in the final against Freddie Tait. And then a hole was played which will always remain as a landmark in the history of the game.

The bunker which guarded the seventeenth green was more than half full of water. Freddie Tait put his second right into the middle of the water. Johnnie Ball played a shot which, personally, I thought was over, but the ominous signal was given "down." When the players arrived on the scene, Freddie Tait's ball was floating, but not floating too well, as it was certainly not quite on the surface of the water, while his opponent's was on the hard sand, between the water and the sleepers.

Freddie walked into the water, which may have been anything between nine to fifteen inches in depth. . . . The shot out could hardly have been improved upon: he ploughed it out on to the green, and oh, the wild shouts that arose!

In the meantime Johnnie Ball had, in my opinion quite as difficult, if not a more difficult, shot to play. He was near the sleepers, and those sleepers are very upright, and the sand on which his ball lay was as hard as adamant. The latter was the difficulty he had to surmount, as it is far from easy to raise a ball quickly from a hard surface; but he did surmount it, as very few men could have done. I do not think that many appreciated what a difficult shot it was, and I have always thought that it has never been quite given its correct value as a wonderful recovery.

Eventually the hole was halved . . . and Ball won at the odd hole.

HAROLD HILTON.

A STUDIOUS middle-aged parson had taken up golf under the tuition of a young enthusiast. For months he foozled every stroke, but at last he hit a "hummer" nearly three hundred yards down the fairway, and his young teacher awaited an outburst of joy. The late beginner slowly picked up his bag. "Have you read Boswell's *Life of Johnson?*" he enquired.

# "AND THOU SHALT WOO HER . . ."

GOLF is a fickle game, and must be wooed to be won. No good can be got by forcing the game; and unless one feels fit and has a keen interest in the match, it is better not to play. It is no use going out and playing around in a half-hearted, listless, indifferent way. Playing in this way is ruinous to good golf. . . .

Further, golf is a business-like game, and should be gone about in a brisk, business-like way. It is far better to play and walk round the links smartly and quickly than to creep round at a snail-like pace. It is impossible to play good golf if you are thinking of something else all the time, and if you have any business worries, leave them behind when you go on the links.

WILLIAM PARK, JUNIOR.

# THE TRIUMVIRATE

NEVER, as leaders at any game, were there three men so closely matched with methods so widely different. You may put that down in large measure, if you please, to the physical, anatomical differences of the three: there was Taylor, short, square, compact, stubby; there was Braid, long, loose-jointed; and there was Vardon, a happy medium between the two, and really a very finely-shaped specimen of a powerful human being.

It is hardly to be questioned which of the three had the most perfect and beautiful style. Vardon lifts up his body a little, away from the ball, as he raises the club. . . . For the rest his style was the perfection of power and ease. Taylor, with the ball opposite the right toe and every stroke played rather on the model generally approved for the half iron shot, had a style as peculiar as his "cobby" build, and specially adapted for it. Braid swung in a loose-jointed way at the ball that did not suggest the mastery and accuracy that he achieved. I doubt whether he played according to any very conscious method. But the results justified the method, or the method-lessness. For a while there was little to choose between these three great ones. But by degrees it became evident that there was a choice: that one was really distinctly better than the other two. Certainly there was a while when Harry Vardon was in a class by himself. For a while he was, I think, two strokes in the round better than either Taylor or Braid and, I believe, better than any other man that we have seen.

HORACE HUTCHINSON.

## THE MASTER STROKE

WHICH is the master stroke in golf? I say that it is the ball struck by any club to which a big pull or slice is intentionally applied for the accomplishment of a specific purpose which could not be achieved in any other way. . . . I call it the master shot because, to accomplish it with any certainty and perfection, it is so difficult even to the experienced golfer; because it calls for the most absolute command over the club and every nerve and sinew of the body, and because, when properly done, it is a splendid thing to see, and for a certainty results in material gain to the man who played it.

HARRY VARDON.

[Clement Flower.

## THE TRIUMVIRATE

*They dominated British golf for twenty years—Harry Vardon (driving),*
*J. H. Taylor (seated), James Braid (standing)*

# THE ANATOMY OF DRIVING

THE whole body must turn on the pivot of the head of the right thigh-bone working in the cotyloidal cavity of the *os innominatum* or pelvic bone; the head, right knee and right foot remaining fixed, with the eyes riveted on the ball. In the upward swing, the vertebral column rotates upon the head of the right femur, the right knee being fixed; and as the club-head nears the ball, the fulcrum is rapidly changed from the right to the left hip, the spine now rotating on the left thigh-bone, the left knee being fixed. . . . Not every professional instructor has succeeded in putting before his pupil the correct stroke in golf in this anatomical exposition. "Juist swoop her awa', maister," says one instructor. "*Hit* ut, mon," says another. Both are right, but such apparently discordant admonitions puzzle the neophyte.

ARNOLD HAULTAIN.

# DEFINITION OF A DRIVER

A DRIVER is an instrument consisting of many parts. It has no legs, but a shaft instead. It has, however, a toe. Its toe is at the end of its face, close to its nose, which is not on its face. Although it has no body, it has a sole. It has a neck, a head, and clubs have horns. They also have a whipping, but this has nothing to do directly with striking the ball. There is little expression in the face of a club. It is usually wooden; sometimes, however, it has a leather face. Clubs, without being clothed, occasionally have lead buttons, but never any button-holes. Clubs' heads are some black, some yellow, but colour is not due to any racial difference. From this description it will be easy to understand, without a diagram, what a driver is like.

SIR WALTER SIMPSON.

I PLAYED a good round against Robert Harris and won, six and five, and then a genial, sandy-haired gentleman, Allan Graham, fairly beat me to death with a queer brass putter.

BOBBY JONES.

# PUTTERS ARE FEMININE

ABOUT the putter there is something so slender and sensitive, so fitful, capricious and fickle, shall I venture to say even at times inconstant, that no doubt can be felt as to the sex question. Plainly, such a companion will not readily be chanced on among the common herd or met with in the crowded street: she must be sought for with care and skill. No club is so human as the putter, none so worthy the name of friend, if true, none more likely to do one an injury if disloyal and treacherous. Like so many of her sex, the putter has a touch of vanity in her nature which must be humoured, if she is to be won as a faithful mistress.

JOHN L. LOW.

THE golfer does not think as he plays his stroke of the hundred and one muscular contractions which, accurately co-ordinated, result in his making a fine drive or a perfect approach. His "sub-liminal self," his "unconscious cerebration," attend to these details without his conscious intervention.

SIR RAY LANKESTER.

# KEEP YOUR EYE ON THE BALL

IF that all-important little rule, Keep your Eye upon the Ball, means anything at all, it means keep it on the ball so that the ball is distinctly seen *and attended to*. One should watch one's ball as a cat watches a mouse. No cat watches a mouse with downcast eyes or with a vacant stare; and no cat, while it watches a mouse, is thinking of anything else.

Golf is more exacting than racing, cards, speculation or matrimony. Golf gives no margin: either you win or you fail. You cannot hedge; you cannot bluff; you cannot give a stop-order; you cannot jilt. One chance is given you, and you hit or miss. There is nothing more rigid in life. And it is this ultra and extreme rigidity that makes golf so intensely interesting.

In almost all other games you pit yourself against a mortal foe; in golf it is yourself against the world: no human being stays your progress as you drive your ball over the face of the globe.

ARNOLD HAULTAIN.

# "FIERY"

THE last of the old line of Musselburgh caddies, John Carey, was familiarly known as "Fiery." His sturdy figure, weather-beaten countenance and inevitable Balmoral bonnet were as familiar as the personality of Willie Park, for whom he caddied. One of the best of the many stories told about him indicated the character of the man and of the race. He was caddying for Park in a match when he was seen wending his solitary way to the club-house. Asked what had happened, "Fiery" said: "A' wanted him to play his iron, and he wud tak' his cleek and we've faun oot."

Accepting a proferred glass of whisky on another occasion, "Fiery" refused soda on the ground that it was "spiling guid drink." On his return from one of his expeditions to the south of England with Park, "Fiery" said of Sandwich that it was so warm "it cudna be very far frae the Saharry Desert." Park himself was responsible for the story that in one of his matches a tee shot struck the pin and lay on the rim. "A bad thing for the caddie," said a bystander. In a moment came the rejoinder from "Fiery": "No' for Park's caddie."

WILLIAM REID.

**"FIERY" (JOHN CAREY)**

*He caddied for Willie Park, the famous*
*Musselburgh golfer, for many years*

# THE CRITIC

I HAD for caddie at Jersey a very small and stolid little boy. Most of the Jersey folk are bi-lingual, but this little boy seemed to have no tongue at all. But towards the end of the round there is, or there was, a hole which was just to be reached by an extra long drive from the tee. I made a very fine drive to this green, and the ball proved to be stone dead, as we came up, just six inches to the right of the hole. And then this astonishing little boy did open his mouth and, still with the solemnity of a cod-fish on his face, ejaculated this comment on what was perhaps the very finest stroke I ever played in my life—"Too much to the roight!"

HORACE HUTCHINSON.

THERE are three classes of people who are entitled to refer to themselves as "We." They are Kings, Editors, and Caddies.

# TWO WAYS OF PUTTING IT

HERE is the same remark in two languages, as told by Sir John Lavery. He was playing at North Berwick and his caddie was betting on him, but he lost the match.

"I am afraid I am not much of a golfer," he said apologetically.

"Ye're not," was the reply.

Not long afterwards he went over to Ireland and the same thing happened. Again he apologised and said he was afraid he was not very good.

"Ah, sure, your honour," said the Irishman. "Faith, few gintlemen can play like you."

\* \* \*

Perhaps the most astonishing reply to a golfer's question was given by a small caddie at Leatherhead.

"How far is this hole, boy?" asked a visitor, as he stood upon the first tee.

"*About five miles from Dorking, sir,*" was the reply.

*From "Candid Caddies."*

# THE CADDIE KNEW BEST . . .

THE accomplishment of a hole in one has called forth a variety of comments from caddies. This happened in Scotland.

After the argument that seems inevitable when Southern players are attended by Scottish caddies, the golfer had decided to take his No. 3 iron at a short hole, the caddie protesting to the end that the shot required a spoon.

Having duly made his "ace," the golfer turned and said: "There you are—you were wrong, you see. A No. 3 was all that was wanted."

"Ye dommed fool," said the caddie. "Ye should have took the spoon. Yon shot will cost ye a poond!"

On another occasion it was a London golfer who performed the feat. After a great deal of argument and not a little acrimony, he had decided on an iron club against the advice of his caddie. In went the ball and "There you are!" he cried triumphantly.

"Yes," said the caddie, "but you'd have done better with a spoon."

*From "Candid Caddies."*

# GOLF PROVERBS

HE'S an unwise pro that beats his only pupil.
    Faint heart never won fair stymie.
      The hole is greater than a half.
The longer the grass, the shorter the temper.
Never say "Dead."
Up all night, down all day.
Putt in haste and repent at leisure.
All holes are blind to those who cannot play.

GERALD BATCHELOR.

CEDRIC SAYNER, once professional at Birkdale, told of a member who was coming up the last hole and asked his caddie what he should take.

"No. 3 iron," the man replied.

The golfer did not believe it, but took the club all the same. He hit a perfect shot and got on the green.

"What made you think I could get there with that?" he asked.

"Well," said the man, "I'd cleaned all the others."

# BOBBY JONES'S YEAR

AMONG years in golf that should have the distinction of extra large red letters, surely 1930 is one. It was supremely dominated by an American, but it will shine for all time in the records of our Championships. It was Bobby Jones's year, when he did the almost unbelievable thing by winning four national championships in a row—the British Amateur and Open, and the corresponding titles in his own country. This was Jones's last "Open," for he retired on the peak of that great year. He was then aged twenty-eight.

FRANK MORAN.

# TOURNAMENT STRAIN

THE strain of championship golf is mostly mental; and certainly the mere physical strain would not burn one up as has been my experience in so many tournaments. Could anyone make me believe that six days of just golf, thirty-six holes a day, would have stripped eighteen pounds off me, as that six days at Oakmont in 1919 did? At Worcester, in the open championship and play-

BOBBY JONES

*The great American amateur in 1930 won the British and American
Open and Amateur Championships—the only man to do so*

off in 1925, I lost twelve pounds in three days. Perhaps these physical symptoms help to explain the furious toll exacted from the spirit under the stress of tournament competition. . . . There are two kinds of golf: golf—and tournament golf. And they are not at all the same thing.

BOBBY JONES.

## "THE HAGE"

MY afternoon at the Meadowbrook Club, near Detroit, was "made" by an incident at its conclusion. Holding court in a corner of the clubhouse, and protesting bitterly at the curious law of the State of Michigan which prohibits the sale of spirits on the Sabbath, was a vast but surely familiar figure.

I had last seen him, about half the present size, descending to the basement of a Carnoustie hotel at two in the morning to cook some trout he had caught during the championship of 1937—the imperishable, unforgettable Walter Hagen.

HENRY LONGHURST.

# PARODIES—AFTER LEWIS CARROLL

SPEAK gruffly to your caddie boy,
   And kick him when he sneezes;
   Your peace of mind he'll else destroy
With grunts and groans and wheezes.

\*   \*   \*

'Twas snowing, yet the wily coves
   Did play and gamble on the links:
All heated were the drying stoves,
   And loud the cry for "Drinks!"

\*   \*   \*

"You are old, Colonel Bogey," the long hitter said,
"And you putt pretty well, though you're never
   quite dead.
I always outdrive you, yet *you*'ve always won;
Will you kindly explain how on earth it is done?"
"Keep your head," said the sage; "don't give up;
   never curse
When conditions are bad, for they might be much
   worse.
If your ball 'lands' in water, sand, shingle or gorse,
Take the rough with the smooth as a 'matter of
   course.' "

GERALD BATCHELOR.

53

# THE EVENING ROUND

THERE is, of course, one ideal method of playing golf on a summer's day, if only the players have time enough, and that is by one morning and one evening round and a long and blissful snooze between lunch and tea. How often have we felt and said, as we start home weary after the day's golf, "Now would be the time to start." There is nothing so heavenly as an evening round when the heat of the day has abated and part of the course is in shadow. Yet we only play that round, as a rule, when it is the only one possible after a day's work in an office. On a holiday we have not always enough self-control to wait for that divine coolness. We pound away in the sun, and when the time comes we are prostrate.

BERNARD DARWIN.

# WHY YOU PLAY GOLF

THE game of golf can be a great builder of character; it can impart something of that peculiar quality known as personality, because it is at once most comprehensive and entirely individualistic. It can be even a selfish game, but there is no reason at all that it should be; rather, the game of golf should be embraced with the intention of joining a great army of good fellows who play it because it is one of the finest forms of outdoor exercise.

HENRY COTTON.

# THE PROPHET

THERE are two young players who have already proved their capabilities and of whom I have big hopes for the future. These are Henry Cotton and Alfred Padgham. Henry Cotton is a very painstaking golfer, one who leaves nothing to chance. His play at times is really wonderful.

HARRY VARDON, in 1933.

# THE SELF-MADE MAN

TO scale the heights in the profession Cotton chose for himself, a man requires two assets —a tough physique and an icy control of his emotions. Cotton had neither. The Cotton of to-day is the perfect example of the self-made man. He "made" his mind and he "made" his body. . . .

His battle with his "temperament" was an interesting study to the man on the touch line, who doesn't have to endure the mental agonies of the player wrestling with the turbulent emotions that surge within him. . . .

Cotton, unlike Hagen, sought complete perfection. Where Hagen, admitting the fallibility of the human make-up, expected four of five execrable shots per round—and made them—Cotton regarded every imperfect stroke as a personal failure. A short putt missed meant, for him, the tortures of the damned. He used to strike himself on the head, quite hard, with his own putter!

I suppose the secret was—and it was certainly part of the secret of his main success—that he was *keen* on golf, keener than any man in Great Britain.

HENRY LONGHURST.

HENRY COTTON

*He won the Open Championship in* 1934, 1937 *and* 1948

# BALLADE OF DEAD GOLFERS

WHERE are the stars that glittered so?
  They wane and flicker, flare and fall;
The champions of long ago
Are hidden 'neath the common pall.
Great Allan of the feathery ball,
  The sandy hair, the carriage staid,
The twinkling eye—beyond recall:
Their race is run, their round is played.

Piries and Parks and Dunns—we know
  They dared the burn and crossed the wall:
Down swooped the rush of time, and lo!
  They vanished in the midnight squall.
Young Tommy, greatest of them all,
  "Thrice belted knight," whose towering shade
Out of the past looms vague and tall—
  Their race is run, their round is played.

The slash, the splendour and the glow,
  The swing that held their foes in thrall,
The sheer perfection of the blow
  Must share the master's funeral.
Yet in their day with great or small,
  Holding their own and unafraid,
They raised their best memorial:
  Their race is run, their round is played.

58

*Envoi*

Prince, ne'er discuss—it breeds but gall—
  How haply they would fare with Braid
In some Elysian carnival:
  Their race is run, their round is played.

BERNARD DARWIN.

## RETROSPECT

WHEN north winds blow,
    And drifting snow
      Spreads o'er the links a mantle white;
    When greens and tees,
    Deserted, freeze,
And waning day soon turns to night;

    In easy chair
    I watch the flare
And flicker of the fitful blaze,
    And in the flames
    Play bygone games,
In visions of soft summer days.

F. B. KEENE.

# AT THE END OF THE YEAR

HOW much does it mean to us, does a year of golf! In the last few moments of the year that you give up to golfing thought and reverie as you sit by the cheerful fire and perhaps, according to the old fancy, toy on the hearthrug for a while with the putter that you hold at convenience in the corner and the memento ball that you preserve upon the mantelpiece—at such time make a pleasant reflection upon all the joy and the gladness, and the health and the adventure, and the glorious rivalry and the close comradeship that have been crowded into this short space of time! Above all, think how much nearer in most blessed friendship has this year of golf drawn you to those who are most after your own heart! There is no habit of man that can do more than golf towards such an end as this, and it is in his abundance of the best friends that a man lives most happily and to the best purpose.

HENRY LEACH.

# THOUGHT AT THE NINETEENTH

WE cannot refrain for the life of us from closing our remarks on golfing with some expression of our intense attachment to it. . . . Golf, thou art a gentle spirit; we owe thee much!

"A KEEN HAND" (H. B. FARNIE).
*From "The Golfer's Manual"* (1857).

# ACKNOWLEDGMENTS

ACKNOWLEDGMENTS are due to the following authors and publishers for the extracts taken from the books named:

*The Spirit of the Links*, by Henry Leach (Methuen).

*The Art of Golf*, by Sir Walter Simpson (Douglas, Edinburgh).

*Concerning Golf*, by J. L. Low (Hodder and Stoughton).

*The Mystery of Golf*, by Arnold Haultain (Macmillan).

*Golf: A Royal and Ancient Game*, by Robert Clark (Macmillan).

*Present-day Golf*, by George Duncan and Bernard Darwin (Hodder and Stoughton).

*Golf*, edited by Horace Hutchinson (Badminton Library; Longmans, Green).

*Golfing Reminiscences*, by William Reid (Gray, Edinburgh).

*Great Golfers in the Making*, edited by Henry Leach (Methuen).

*Golfers' Gallery*, by Frank Moran (Oliver and Boyd).

*Golf Stories*, by Gerald Batchelor (A. and C. Black).

*Candid Caddies*, by Charles Graves and Henry Longhurst (Duckworth).

*Fifty Years of Golf*, by Horace Hutchinson (Country Life).

*My Golfing Reminiscences*, by Harold Hilton (Nisbet).

*The Complete Golfer*, by Harry Vardon (Methuen).

*The Game of Golf*, by W. Park, Jr. (Longmans, Green).

*Down the Fairway*, by Robert T. Jones and O. B. Keeler (Allen and Unwin).

*Tee Shots and Others*, by Bernard Darwin (Kegan Paul).

*Golfing Memories and Methods*, by Joyce Wethered (Hutchinson).

*It was Good while it Lasted*, by Henry Longhurst (Dent).

*Golf*, by Henry Cotton (Eyre and Spottiswoode).

*Rubs of the Green*, by Bernard Darwin (Chapman and Hall).

*Golfing Reminiscences*, by Mabel E. Stringer (Mills and Boon).

*Lyrics of the Links*, by F. B. Keene (Cecil Palmer).

*The Golfer's Manual*, by "A Keen Hand" (Dropmore Press).

*Golf between Two Wars*, by Bernard Darwin (Chatto and Windus).